THE ENGLISH GENTLEMAN
ABROAD

THE ENGLISH GENTLEMAN ABROAD

Douglas Sutherland

PREFACE BY
HIS GRACE THE DUKE OF ST ALBANS

DRAWINGS BY
TIMOTHY JAQUES

BURKE'S PEERAGE LTD

Text © Douglas Sutherland 1984
Illustrations © Timothy Jaques 1984
Published by Burke's Peerage Ltd
1 Hay Hill, London W1X 7LF

ISBN 0 85011 042 4

Printed and bound in Great Britain
at The Pitman Press, Bath

Foreword

BY HIS GRACE THE DUKE OF ST ALBANS

High time for a book on this fascinating and intriguing subject. Having spent quite a large slice of my life in foreign parts, I am not only interested, but personally concerned in the subject — and who better to write about it than Douglas Sutherland, the greatest living authority on the species and his habits?

As a child I had a mole's eye view of the breed in France, Germany and Belgium. After school, back again as a student in Germany and France. Then the rather special war and post-war "officer-and-gentleman" period in North Africa, Italy and finally five years in Austria.

Now from my base in Monte Carlo, as I do a lot of travelling, I can follow the gentleman's development in the 1980s on a fairly world-wide basis.

For me the prototype has always been my father who, despite spending almost his entire life up to the age of sixty in the Colonies — South Africa and Canada — betrayed no detectable signs of ever having deserted the shores of Britain. This despite the fact that, due to some careless family planning, he was born in Brussels in the year 1850.

Reluctantly he spent most of the '20s on the Continent. Nearly half a decade in France, a year in Belgium and a couple of years in Germany never encouraged in him the gift of tongues. In fact I never

heard him utter a single word in French or German — and among his contemporaries he was not alone in this. Not out of arrogance, for he was a diffident man. He just thought that English was the obvious language for communication and he had considerable sympathy for those who had been brought up to speak less satisfactory tongues. Conversation with non-English speaking foreigners was inevitably limited — though not greatly missed — and he always seemed to obtain the services he required.

I should perhaps add that his appearance, if not typically English, certainly struck an exotic note in the countries he patronised. A Homburg hat, a mustard-coloured cloak with a scarlet lining and a silver-topped cane, combined to arouse in me the maximum reactions of shame and embarrassment!

His generation was followed by a far more self-conscious lot. Foreign languages might be spoken, albeit usually badly and with an execrable accent. The supreme degree of self-assurance had gone with the Empire.

Today the English gentleman's discomfiture may plumb new depths. "But we thought the English were gentlemen," they say with relish, having unearthed a specimen in his low-profile residence, and referring to enthusiastic and literally bloody English football fans pictured by the international press, *bloody but unbowed* as they are escorted to the hospitality of some foreign cooler under police escort.

Personally, I have always found that, even before opening my mouth, I am regularly recognized as belonging to the island race. Whether this is for physical or vestimentary reasons, I do not know. Once I give tongue, it can be another matter. On a recent visit to Arizona a charming waitress enquired what sort of an accent mine was. I pointed out that it was she and not I who had an accent!

"Oh — I guess you must be Australian".

Enough said. I leave it to the witty and practised pen of Douglas Sutherland to enlarge upon the hazards encountered by the English gentleman who is rash or brave enough to venture abroad in the age of travel for the masses.

Introduction

I have remarked in another place that English gentlemen do not really go abroad very much except in time
of war. I have also said somewhere else that English
gentlemen 'invented' abroad.

These seemingly contradictory statements are, in
fact, easily reconcilable.

That the English gentleman invented abroad is, of
course, not open to contradiction. 'Abroad' in this
context does not mean places such as India or Africa
or other parts of the Empire (dec'd) which were quite
a different matter. English gentlemen went there as a
matter of duty with the laudable desire of ameliorat-
ing the condition of the people almost (but not quite)
as much as with the very proper ambition of lining
their own pockets.

Abroad, in the sense in which it is used in the title of
this manual, means such countries as gentlemen
repair to from time to time for no other purpose than
to enjoy themselves (or, as in the case of war, to
protect their right to continue to do so).

By and large this means countries such as France
and Switzerland, small parts of Spain and Portugal,
and even smaller parts of Belgium — fashions, of
course, change. There was a time when to visit Italy
was an essential part of a gentleman's education, but
not so much now since it has assumed a strange politi-

cal hue, and anyway took the wrong side in the last war. Greece was never held in much regard after Lord Elgin had bagged their marbles, and Egypt even less so since Lord Carnarvon succumbed to the Curse of Tutankhamun.

There are, of course, notable exceptions to these generalities. There are still some mildly eccentric gentlemen who enjoy spending time sitting up to their necks in evil-smelling mud in places like Baden-Baden, or drinking even more evil-smelling water at Evian in France. Quite a few also go to selected islands such as Corfu, in spite of its being Greek, not, let it be understood, for the climate or to gaze at the newly-acceptable nudity on its beaches, but to play cricket or to visit the English Cemetery.

It is also true to say that abroad has gone considerably out of fashion since the days of the Grand Tour, which was anyway largely considered educational.

To journey abroad in pursuit of pleasure has also considerably declined since the pioneering days when the English first conceived the idea of sliding down alps on two narrow strips of board, ducking themselves in the waters of the Mediterranean (an idea quite abhorrent at the time to the natives) or treading in the footsteps of Edward VII who, when Prince of Wales, put it about quite fallaciously that ladies on the other side of the Channel threw off their inhibitions and their clothes much more readily than their English counterparts.

The Great Revival

While the above observations are a fairly accurate survey of the gentleman's attitude to abroad since the rollicking days of *la fin de siècle*, there is now very strong evidence indeed that attitudes are changing sharply. Quite why this should be so is not altogether clear, although one might hazard a guess or two.

Probably one major factor is that the opportunities for pursuing their traditional sports and pastimes in their homeland are becoming ever more restricted.

Take grouse shooting, for example. The once traditional exit of '*le tout Londres*' after Goodwood to open fire on the Scottish moors on the 12th of August is dwindling to a trickle. Every year there are fewer and fewer Scottish lairds who can afford to hold out against the blandishments of the wealthy syndicates. As one gentleman of my acquaintance put it: 'Who wants to go all that way just to risk being shot at by a lot of strangers?'

Much the same applies to salmon fishing, where the number of salmon running up the rivers is in decreasing proportion to the mounting cost of trying to catch them.

Then again it has to be admitted that there is an increasing number of gentlemen who are not their own masters. The time when a gentleman's progress through each year was inescapably governed by the social calendar is largely over.

Time was when gentlemen never went on holiday, as the word is generally understood. He went to places at the same time every year to *do* something, be it fox-hunting or horse-racing, salmon-fishing or pheasant-shooting. Each followed each other as certainly as spring followed winter.

Today the great majority have to agonize over what they must cut out, and seek to find what is most to their taste in the time they have at their disposal.

It is for those who are turning to rediscovering the tastes of their forebears by journeying abroad that I have carefully researched this book.

Of course, a work of this scope and magnitude could not possibly have been achieved without a great deal of help from friends more experienced in certain parts of the world of expanding horizons for the

gentleman now travelling abroad than I could ever become. Some of these I have acknowledged in the text. To those who have made their contributions unsung I am equally grateful.

That the advice which I am able to offer is largely for the benefit of English gentlemen, their wives, children and other appendages is not something for which I apologise. They have their special needs and motivations and their own ideas of what constitutes foreign travel which are often far removed from those perhaps more worldly-wise who know exactly how to go about getting their chips-with-everything.

Benidorm, 1984

How to get there

In the days when the English Channel was the English Channel and the only way to get abroad was to cross it in a boat, it was generally considered by we British as a stretch of water provided by Providence to insulate us from the necessity to fraternize with the blackies, who, by general consensus of opinion, started at Calais.

When William the Conqueror made his one-way crossing with his band of mercenaries none of them showed the slightest desire to return to the badlands of Normandy whence they had come, although in more recent times a number of otherwise xenophobic English families proudly claim to be descended from them — rather like all those malcontents who made the crossing to the New World in search of something or another in what would appear to have been a grossly overcrowded *Mayflower*.

Before the strange whim affected certain members of the British aristocracy to go on a Grand Tour of Inspection to see how *les autres* were getting along, there were few gentlemen who gave abroad a second thought. There was a certain Captain Webb who *swam* the English Channel in his longjohn swimming costume but his feat was so little regarded at the time that his only lasting memorial is a brand of matches named after him.

Indeed there was something rather suspicious

about anyone showing a desire to go the other way, like spendthrift Regency bucks fleeing their creditors, or Oscar Wilde, ostracized by Society, retreating to an attic in Paris to die beyond his means.

Apart from the periodic forays of our Armies to the Continent to discourage actual or potential disturbers of the peace the Cross-Channel traffic was never very heavy and was confined largely to the upper echelons of Society.

In fact, in 1939 there were only two paddle steamers plying between Dover and Calais. I can well remember, at a rather grand diplomatic occasion in the late 1930's, overhearing a delightful snatch of conversation between an elderly lady of obviously teutonic origins and a true blue-blooded English gentleman.

Evidently the lady had not circulated in diplomatic circles long enough to recognize the species, for I heard her ask earnestly:

"For how long haff you been in Engeland?"

"Madam," said the English Gentleman, drawing himself up to his full height and looking down his patrician nose, "my family came over with William the Conqueror."

"Ah," said the lady sadly. "What a pity we are missing each other. We came over with the *Maid of Kent*", which was, of course, the name of the *other* paddle steamer.

Dear me! How all that has changed now. To look at one of those maps which chart the cross-channel ferries is almost as confusing and bewildering as a tracing of the shunting yards at Crewe. Add to this the Armada of airplanes which roars daily out of Gatwick, Heathrow and all places North heading for all places South, each packed to the emergency exits with eager trippers headed for the most recently developed

Blackpool-sur-Mer and it will be readily realized that things are not all what they used to be.

Faced with this democratization of what was once almost exclusively the playtime of the upper classes, it has to be said that they have adapted with surprising resilience.

Perhaps their espousal of the airplane as a method of travel demonstrates this as much as anything. The old-fashioned brigade, of course, have never come fully to terms with the unnatural business of aircraft jetting off almost vertically without even a propeller in sight. Pre-war there were certain intrepid individuals who would roar across the Channel, helmeted and goggled, in incredibly small aeroplanes with their golf clubs in the back and a girl on their knee for a dashing weekend at Le Touquet, but that was about the limit of it.

Today, although almost any form of travel is preferred to the airplane, there are many gentlemen who have come to accept it as inevitable in a modern world.

Not all, however, have come to terms with the amenities of air travel. Take for example the matter of the sanitary arrangements, something with which gentlemen travelling abroad are greatly pre-occupied.

The gentleman is accustomed to the facilities available on the railway, probably still his favourite form of travel. Warned by the familiar notice "Passengers are requested not to flush the toilet whilst the train is standing in a station", they assiduously refrain from doing so, conscious that the resultant jetsam on the railway line would be offensive to those remaining on the platform after the train has moved out. With the train speeding through the countryside it is quite a different matter.

Consider now the plight of the gentleman brought up to be considerate at all times to others, when using the 'facilities' while flying high over friendly territory.

*A friend of the author depicted at his club, recounting
tales of his exploits abroad – and none better all are
agreed – especially with a glass of
Armagnac de Montal – and the bottle near to hand*

Armagnac de MONTAL

To refrain from flushing and so risk giving offence to the next user of the aerial thunderbox or to flush and risk a direct hit on a perambulating peasant below is a dilemma which only a lengthy course of de-briefing of the train-orientated traveller can resolve.

There are many other problems facing the pre-space age traveller which bewilder and confuse, from the limitation imposed by financial consideration on the number of heavy leather trunks to be taken to the improbable provision of small brown paper sick bags for use in emergency — the gentleman has been accustomed since time immemorial to use his (or somebody else's) hat.

That the younger generation, uninhibited by the reservations of their fathers, have taken so enthusiastically to jet-setting around the world is something that was explained to me recently by a noted psychiatrist who has made a study of this sort of thing. For the post-war generation travel by air is not at all menacing. On the contrary it is equated with their childhood days in the nursery when all was warm and secure. Once aboard one of these vast aircraft the air hostess, fussing around to satisfy every whim, becomes a nanny figure, only more so, to the sexually emerging adolescent. The fastening of the seat belt is symbolic of being tucked up in bed and the appearance of those little individual plastic trays laden with their favourite junk foods is like having their supper brought to them in the nursery. Thus the belly of the airplane satisfies all their back-to-the-nursery yearnings.

Be that as it may, what is unquestionable is that the acceptance of the airplane as a mode of travel has greatly widened the frontiers of abroad-minded gentlemen. Places of nostalgic memory like Ceylon now called something else (Sri Lanka. Ed.) and many other places not so long ago painted red on the map of the world are no longer reached only after weeks of pleasurable cruising and romantic dalliance with handsome ship's officers or gay grass widows, according to taste. Today you can be in the far pavilions of the Empire-that-was almost before you can undo your seat belt, so it is probably right in this survey of the opportunities open to the modern traveller to include some expert advice on adventures of this sort. For this purpose I have enlisted the help of those more familiar than I with such places and their dispatches will be found in the second part of this volume.

I have also included observations on travel to the United States of America. I leave it to the reader to decide whether the behaviour of our ex-colonists at a certain tea-party in Boston should be so far forgotten as to permit of their inclusion in what is undoubtedly a very upper-crust survey of potential playgrounds the world over.

What to Take

One of the English gentleman's strong points is planning. The old Army axiom that time spent in reconnaisance is seldom wasted has been well and truly drummed into him and he in turn has drummed into those of his family over whom he manages to exert any control the importance of anticipating difficulties, recognizing them in time and taking the necessary steps to surmount them. Whether it be a pheasant shoot, his daughter's wedding or simply a couple of days in London he will devote the same amount of care to planning.

The symptoms, generally known as 'nesting', are easily recognized. He will spend a great deal of time pacing with measured tread up and down the terrace, hands clasped behind his back, while he works out the main strategy. This is followed by a period seated at his desk in his study gazing at a clip-board covered with pristine white sheets of paper and a freshly sharpened pencil. He will also have an india rubber (bungee) which he uses with great frequency. English gentlemen always work in pencil as they always rub, never cross, anything out, something they have learned from years of doing the *Times* crossword. He will also have a large magnifying glass, which he never uses, and a handbell, which he only uses in emergency, like calling for somebody to re-sharpen his pencil.

In planning anything as momentous as a trip abroad the time occupied by this stage is very great indeed. It is also generally conducted in an atmosphere of secrecy. To have half the neighbourhood know what he is up to would never do at all, although he might call upon the services, as an expert adviser, of somebody who had been before to wherever he is going. He may also issue a stand-by order to his wife or any others of his family who might be involved, but there will seldom be joint consultation. After all he is going for his own amusement, not theirs.

The Medicine Chest

With any luck the Great Planner will have the advantage of certain short cuts. One of these is that he will probably have as a family heirloom a list of the contents of the medicine chest taken by his great-great-grandfather to the Crimea or by nearer forebears on later military campaigns. It will not occur to him to vary the contents, other than marginally, if some of the standard medications of former times are no longer available.

Great care is taken with the medicine chest because gentlemen are generally of the opinion that foreign doctors are not up to much and foreign dentists beyond the pale. He will have heard travellers' tales of the enormous sums of money exacted from those

reporting sick abroad and, in this at least, he will not have been incorrectly informed.

Gentleman, by their nature, are singularly prone to toothache on account of their aversion to buying toothpaste, preferring a good scrubbing with cold water. The standard remedy for toothache has, since time immemorial, been a product with the brand name of 'Nervine' made by the firm of Bunter. Bunter's Nervine dropped into the cavity is a miraculous pain-killer, although care must be taken that the frequent draughts of whisky which follow as part of the treatment do not wash it all out again before it can take effect.

There are a number of other well-known medicines available at all good chemists, without the necessity of a National Health prescription, which have stood the test of time. Pre-eminent is Doctor Collis Brown's mixture for upset stomachs and, perhaps more essentially, as a cure for the excesses of the night before. This used to come wrapped in a testimonial from none other than Sir Edward Whypmer, the first man to climb the Matterhorn. Alas, with the last bottle I bought this impressive evidence of its effectiveness was no longer included. I hope this is not a sign of yet another break with tradition.

In the same category, but more in favour with the gentler sex, are Carter's Little Liver Pills, which used to be widely advertised as 'The Pink Pills for Pale People'. Another peculiarly feminine stand-by is *sal volatile*, which many ladies of quality still carry in their handbags against the keenly-looked-forward-to moment when they will meet a tall dark stranger and feel weak at the knee.

Less romantic, but possibly more practical, are the many correctives of the bodily functions. Beecham's Powders (*not* pills) and Cascara Evacuant remain strong favourites with grown-ups, while either Ex-Lax or Syrup of Figs should be included if there are children to be considered.

Accidents are taken care of with bandages of various widths, lint, iodine, peroxide and sharp scissors.

Deficiencies which seem common to all foreign apothecaries necessitate the inclusion of items like Carbolic Soap, Izal and Derris Powder, while all gentlemen consider it wise to travel with their own supply of lavatory paper, that supplied in even the most elegant of foreign hotels being in no way considered a substitute for the best of British Bronco.

Quantities considered necessary vary marginally from area to area. For example, generally speaking the amount of lavatory paper required increases the further south one adventures, the theory being that the nearer you get to Egypt the more likely you are to contract Gippy Tummy, more generally known as Tutankhamun's Revenge.

By the same token there are certain items which are only essential in certain climates. For example to go fishing in Norway without anti-chill medicines such as Friar's Balsam (remember to bring your own sugar lumps if taken orally rather than as an inhalant), or Zubes for the children to suck would be as short-sighted as to travel in Spain without extra stocks of fly repellant. Stuff to deal with mosquitoes should be taken *everywhere*, but anti-rabies serum, quinine for tsetse fly or the antidote for scorpion bites can be cut to the minimum north of the English Channel.

Of course this is only an indication of some of the decision-making and planning required before setting out for abroad. There are many other weighty matters which must be given careful consideration. Take, for example, the wardrobe.

The Wardrobe

Of all items, hats possibly give a gentleman most to

A Gentleman abroad is deserted by Lady Luck at the tables. Silly importunate man to seek such an extreme, not to say final, solution – with the telephone waiting to connect him to Christie's – and his wife's jewels still glistening warm round her neck.

CHRISTIE'S
LONDON

Christie's, 8 King Street, St. James's, London SW1Y 6QT.
Telephone: (01) 839 9060, Telex: 916429

worry about, especially if he is going somewhere he has not been before; he feels the most frightful ass wearing the wrong hat. A 'boater' is perfectly *comme il faut* when strolling along the Promenade des Anglais in Nice but highly inappropriate for visiting the tomb of the Unknown Warrior in Paris, however hot it may be. It is really bowler hats for visiting old battlefields, tweed caps for any sporting activity in other parts of the interior and boaters for the seaside, except in the evening when a white or brown velour is appropriate. A gentleman is wise to restrict himself to such bare essentials as these because it enables him to insist that his wife do the same. It should also be remembered that porters are often very difficult to come by nowadays, even abroad, and hat boxes are the very devil to deal with on one's own.

Jackets present much the same problem as hats. Gentlemen do not go out in shirtsleeves abroad any more than they would do at home, except in the most exceptional circumstances. A gentleman's wardrobe consists almost entirely of jackets.

Other Equipment

There was a time when to travel abroad entailed taking absolutely everything which might be needed. The impossibility of acquiring by local purchase such necessities as a moustache curler or one of those knives-with-a-gadget-for-taking-stones-out-of-horses-hooves are long since over. It is now, for example, quite unnecessary to take that purely English invention, the bucket and spade, to the seaside, since those devilishly ingenious Japanese have flooded the civilized world with replicas almost indistinguishable from the originals.

That times can change like this is something which is not readily grasped by some. For example, I can well remember when it was foolhardy in the extreme to venture into the mountains of Switzerland without a carefully checked survival kit. It was carried in pouches strapped round the middle and consisted of an electric torch (with spare batteries), candles, matches, string, needle and thread, brandy, a Bulldog Drummond novel by Sapper, a boy scout knife as aforesaid and much else besides.

Nowadays the more with-it visitors to the ski slopes affect a rather more stylish version of these old-fashioned holdalls with rather more practical contents like haversack rations, a copy of *Playboy* and the latest in prophylactics.

Recently I had occasion to challenge a fellow down-hill dasher in the most jocular way about the contents of his ditty-bag. With earnest concentration he started to name each object as he produced it for inspection: "An electric torch (with spare batteries) candles, matches......" The only indication that he was moving with the times was that the novel was by Ian Fleming. This is carrying tradition too far.

Nevertheless, abroad cannot be relied upon to pro-duce items of equipment of a more specialized nature. Times may change but many of the old standards still prevail. For instance the precept that it is simply not done for a friend to ask a gentleman to lend him his horse, his gun or his wife is still generally accepted, though nowadays the wife may be running a rather poor third.

Still less would a gentleman hire a gun or a fishing rod or whatever else of a personal nature he might need to do whatever he has gone abroad for. Thus a gentleman going abroad to shoot things would cer-tainly require to take his own cartridges, which in turn means bringing along an enormously heavy cartridge box which often weighs heavier than its contents, not to mention an assortment of clothing, hats and boots, so that he is apt to finish up with a trousseau of such

*The English Gentleman treats Ballantine's Finest
Scotch Whisky
with the calm and deliberation it commands.*

Ballantine's

HIRAM WALKER & SONS (SCOTLAND) PLC
3 HIGH STREET, DUMBARTON,
SCOTLAND G82 1ND   TELEPHONE 0389 6511

proportions as to force his wife to travel with a single light suitcase and to rule out any possibility of making the journey by air.

Luggage

The trouble with a gentleman's luggage is that it is all made of very solid leather which weighs a ton even when empty. His hat box for example (see *Wardrobe*) will be a survival from the days of the British Raj and originally intended for carrying his solar topée. The box has survived long after the army of bearers has departed. As the English gentleman never throws anything away he will use it for his hard hats such as the bowler, which the French rather rudely call *le chapeau melon*. Such pieces of luggage which are not leather will be japanned tin trunks designed to frustrate the efforts of termites. Both tin trunks and leather cases will be inscribed with the name of some long dead forebear and carry such legends as 'Not Wanted On Voyage', 'Elder Demster' or 'White Star Shipping Line', in addition to labels for such destinations as Bombay, Singapore, Cape Town or Shanghai. It is not difficult to discover when one is travelling in the company of a gentleman, even if only making the crossing to Calais.

The Responsibility

The most cursory perusal of the foregoing will give the reader some idea of the weight of responsibility which lies on the shoulders of a gentleman planning a trip abroad. He can expect little or no help from his wife in these matters. While she might reasonably be expected to get her own wardrobe together there is no guarantee that in the excitement of the moment she will not forget things which are clearly in her department like the bridge cards, or even a supply of marmalade (short-term visits should also allow for one's personal stock of kippers).

Unless the gentleman spends much time on his check lists and personally supervises the packing, nothing but disaster can ensue.

*"Oh how frightfully clever, George! – isn't it our
Bank Manager?"*

From Pall Mall (London, Eng.) to Pasadena (Calif., U.S. of A.)
Lloyds Bank remains at the service of
the English Gentleman abroad – or at home – in 47 countries

Who to take

The hardest wrench for anyone about to embark for abroad is leaving the dogs behind. It seems, on the face of it, most unfair that you can take anything from your horse to the children's white mice but no dogs. Of course you *can* take your dog across the Channel should you so wish. The trouble is that you have to put him in six months' quarantine when you want to bring him back again. Attempts to smuggle him past the Customs under milady's petticoats are almost certainly doomed to failure, especially if he is a Great Dane or even, as is more likely, a labrador.

Anti-canine discrimination apart, who you choose to take is up to you. It is the general experience that it is as stupid to take your mistress abroad as it would be to take a bottle of wine to a restaurant which charges excessively high prices for corkage.

Equally there is not much point in taking servants of any description, since there are few establishments nowadays which will bed them down in the stables for a modest charge and feed them on scully.

So that really means that you are stuck with your wife and such children as you cannot dispose of elsewhere.

Conversation Abroad

The general rule that the Englishman at home would rather die than address a remark, even in a first class railway carriage, to a fellow traveller, is, by tacit agreement, abided by.

An even more firmly entrenched rule is that the closer a neighbour is in terms of geography, the less proper it is to indulge in any form of meaningful dialogue. Thus cheek-by-jowl householders who have lived next door to each other for a quarter of a century would not consider that sufficient reason to raise their hats should they chance to encounter each other in the street.

Communication between neighbours, be it on the same down train to London or next-door houses in Chelsea, is only permissible in (a) times of emergency like a rail strike or England threatened with having to follow on in the final Test at the Oval, or (b) a declaration of war. The exception to this is when abroad.

The odd thing about gentlemen abroad is not only that they lose their inhibitions about addressing their fellow countrymen despite their being complete strangers but that they almost feel it incumbent upon themselves to do so.

Certainly they do not go so far as flashing their lights or waving out of car windows when they spot another G.B. number plate, like football club suppor-

*A dear and rather potty old friend of the author seen
pacifying the natives during his travels abroad. It is
clear they will have none of his beads and much prefer
the real thing, which is exclusive and individually
made, to be found only at Charles de Temple,
52 Jermyn Street, London SW1*

CHARLES DE TEMPLE

ters when they recognize their club's coloured scarf streaming from the back of another car swerving up the motorway. However, should they chance on one of their own sort in a hotel or even espy one at the next table in a restaurant, the urge to communicate is immediate and overpowering.

Nor is it a matter of merely indulging in a few pleasantries such as "Where have you come from?" or "Where are you going?". They appear to be afflicted with a sudden and intense interest in their new acquaintances to whom they would not dream of giving the time of day if met with on home ground.

The symptoms are understandably more acute should one chance to fall in with a resident member of one of the many English communities which are dotted all over Europe and far beyond. These beleaguered souls, wearing the hair shirt of the exile from the homeland to which they will not (and indeed, in not a few cases, cannot) return are as avid for news of home as they are curious about whoever has been fortuitously thrust into their company.

Whether it be the *oiseau de passage* or the exile, the rules of the game are the same, though in the case of the exile rather more so.

The essence of the game is to extract every tittle of information about the other's tastes, friends and social and financial status while at the same time ensuring that you yourself are superior on all counts.

It is a game which requires the greatest subtlety and skill to play successfully. The prize is to part on an eternal oath of eternal friendship and, unless by some unhappy accident, never to meet again. It is only possible in the limited compass of this book to give the sketchiest outline of the rules.

Opening gambits

After the first introductions have been effected it is

not done to discuss the weather. The weather will almost certainly be exactly the same as it was the previous day in any case. The bull question is "Have you heard what the rate of exchange is today?"

This is intended to establish you immediately as someone of financial consequence to whom even the most fractional rise or drop in the franc, mark, peseta or what-have-you is a matter of the greatest moment and might require immediate action on the wire.

If your opponent is worth his salt he will come up with something like: "Bank offered me 220 this morning. Didn't take it. If Thatcher gets her foot on the neck of the EEC today we'll be in for an improvement. I'd hold off if I were you."

What you are both discussing, of course, is whether or not to cash £50 worth of travellers' cheques where a move of one point either way might make a difference of 50p, but honour will have been satisfied and you can settle down to weightier business.

In the meantime your wife should be batting strongly on her own wicket. The sort of remark you might overhear in the Ladies Gossip Stakes should go something like: "As I was saying to my under-gardener just before we left.....".

Always, note, the *under*-gardener. How else is anyone to know that you keep two gardeners? There is no reason to disclose that you got the lad for nothing through the Youth Opportunities Scheme and that the 'head' gardener is retired on half-pay anyway. It is one of the rules of the game to tell the truth but not necessarily all the truth.

Here are some further examples of useful openings: "It's terribly sad, but I really will have to retire old Sarah. She's getting awfully slow. Do you know, it now takes her all day just to clean the dining-room silver."

It is not old Sarah's deficiencies which are of

The finest tableware for the finest food both at home and abroad – The English Gentleman thinks it would have been better to have stayed at home!

Royal Doulton

interest but the amount of dining-room silver there is to be cleaned.

Servants and their strengths and shortcomings are fertile ground in which to plant the seeds which will establish social status.

To have it known that nanny is getting quite impossible in her old age, seldom leaving her room, expecting to be cooked for and waited on hand and foot by the other servants is to establish at one blow that one has a whole heirarchy of servants.

Similarly a passing reference to grooms, keepers or ghillies comfortably establishes ownership of many acres and opens the door to asking how many pheasants one's opponent shot on the opening day. It is to the other's discomfiture, of course, if it reveals that he has neither pheasants nor acres. In this case it is likely to be game, set and match to you. The only way he can get back into contention is by complaining of the headaches of having his house open to the public or running a Safari Park in the grounds.

These are extreme cases, since the likelihood of two established members of the landed gentry meeting up in some corner of a foreign field is remote in the extreme. They are too busy totting up the gate money at home and too mean to spend it horsing around abroad.

The rest of us must be content with establishing *bona fides* with far less impressive credentials and here the secret is never to overplay one's hand.

The chap who complains of the cost of leaving his Rolls Royce in the long-stay car park at the airport is blundering into a minefield. Few with any pretentions to social position would own anything so ostentatious as a Rolls and, if by chance he did, would tend to apologize for it rather than boast about it.

A gaucherie of this sort also lays open he who commits it to the simplest of counterpunches, which might go something like: "I always have my man drop me off. One needs somebody to cope with the luggage anyway" and at once establishes that one keeps a manservant, leaving an ugly suspicion hanging in the air that the other fellow has not. Having a manservant carries far more points in the league table than having a Rolls and humping your own bags.

The female version of getting the foot on the neck, as the Rolls Royce owner's wife, struggling to establish that she buys her underwear at Janet Reger, under the pretext of complaining about the price, might find her wondering where she went wrong when met with a sympathetic rejoinder like: "It must be awfully difficult for you, my dear. Personally I always wear Henry's."

Peaceful relations can only be established with one side being declared the outright winner whereupon they all become the best of friends. All good clean fun and at least it saves having to struggle to make oneself understood by people who don't speak English.

Hints for Gentlemen Travelling
by Air

Although an earlier chapter touched on some of the problems of air travel, it is such a comparatively new development that, before we examine the habits and customs of gentlemen in faraway places, it might be helpful to give a résumé of some of the new know-how of air travel and the gentleman's developing skill in adapting to it.

At the Airport

It should be noted that there is a regulation with regard to air travel which requires passengers to be at the airport one hour before boarding.

At first sight this would appear to be no hardship. Gentlemen undertaking a train journey of any distance customarily arrive at the station long before the advertised departure time. This enables them to make arrangements for the comfort of their dogs during the journey, seeing that their luggage is properly distributed between their carriage and the guard's van and selecting suitable reading matter for the journey, before settling themselves comfortably in their reserved seat on the train which will already be standing in the station.

Travel by air is quite another matter. In the first

place the authorities, having got all their passengers marshalled at the airport an hour before kick-off, display the utmost reluctance in allowing them actually to board the aircraft until the last minute. This can be for a number of reasons, one of which is that the aircraft has not yet arrived from wherever it is coming. Others are that they are checking to see if it has any petrol in it, that the pilot has overslept or that they are all hanging about for the drummer of some pop group to be mobbed all the way to the reception area reserved for Very Important Persons.

Whatever the reason, the gentleman traveller, embarrassed by the selection of magazines on the bookstalls almost exclusively featuring naked ladies, at the expense of magazines like *The Field* and *The Shooting Times* and even in many cases the daily newspapers, will, if he knows what's good for him, make his way to the duty-free lounge where he will be entitled to buy himself a drink no matter what hour of the day. Thereafter the aircraft can please itself when it takes off.

Such are the frustrations of travel by air.

Class Conscious

While a gentleman from force of habit always travels first class by boat and train, the advent of air travel has not apparently imposed the same superstition.

This is because, given the chance of sharing first-class exclusivity with pop groups, stars of stage, screen and radio and toothpaste salesmen travelling on expense accounts, he prefers to throw in his lot with the common herd.

For the same reason he tends to shun travel by Concorde, and, should he do so he, certainly would not boast about it. In earlier times travellers to India and the East used to specify Port Out, Starboard Home so

"*We not only managed to trace your ancestors,
Mr Smith, but a branch of the family you may not
have known about!*"

Your ancestor too?

Burke's Peerage 1 Hay Hill London W1

"Smithson? Be a good chap. Pop over the road would you, and get a case of the Good Ordinary Claret?"

BERRY BROˢ. & RUDD Lᵀᴰ

Wine and Spirit Merchants
3 St. James's Street London SW1
and The Wine Shop Houndmills Basingstoke Hants.

that their cabins would benefit from the maximum shade both ways. This gave rise to the rather sneering description of travelling 'Posh' and smacked of the nouveau rich.

Before Mr Laker's lamented demise as a cheap flight operator those wishing to cause the greatest social impact on arrival in New York were wont to travel C.O.L.B. which had much the same connotations. It stood for Concorde Out, Laker Back. Gentlemen never travelled C.O.L.B.

Patriotism

On the whole a gentleman will travel by a British airline, all other things being equal and providing he does not have one of those dreadful little canvas shoulder bags forced on him advertising the airline and supposed to carry some sort of social cachet. In the same way he would not dream of travelling Pan Am simply to qualify as a member of the Pan Am Clipper Club. Nor would he choose Lufthansa simply because he finds it unnerving when the pilot uses the line of the Thames as a landmark. Memories of war time air raids die hard.

Not club material

It has been remarked that if two or more English gentlemen meet in however remote a part of the world, their first instinct is to form a club. This does not apply to the English gentleman travelling by air even to the extent of his eschewing the V.I.P. lounge on the grounds that those who take advantage of these sort of facilities are not the sort of people he wants to mix with.

Still less is he liable to claim membership of the Mile High Club the qualification for which appears to be to have performed some unmentionable sexual rite more than one mile above the earth's surface.

All in all the shared dangers of air travel do not induce in the English Gentleman a feeling of togetherness with his fellows as it would appear to do with lesser mortals. Certainly he would not join in the relieved round of applause traditionally accorded to the Captain by the package tourists when he brings their craft safely to earth.

On the other hand should he encounter the Captain whilst disembarking he has been known to shake him fervently by the hand in a silent act of thanksgiving for his deliverance.

"Oh my God, do-it-yourself caviar! – If we'd never come abroad we could have stayed in London and had the real thing."

SCOTTS

20 MOUNT STREET LONDON W1   01-629 5248

Letters from Spain

When Alice Burlington told my wife of plans my old friend Bobby was making to take her on a longish trip to Spain I was both surprised and pleased. Surprised because Bobby, an inveterate visitor to the battlefields of France, was showing a bit of the pioneering spirit in this new venture and pleased because it seemed to offer an opportunity of observing the reactions of an English gentleman abroad in a country where the species have not been identified in any considerable numbers since the Peninsular Wars.

I begged of Alice that she write a blow-by-blow account of the experience, and this she readily agreed to do. For allowing me to publish the letters which follow I would like to offer her my sincere gratitude.

* * *

Dear Mary,

Well here we are ploughing through the Bay of Biscay although I am glad to say it is not at all rough.

Bobby is in an absolutely *foul* temper and I must confess that I don't altogether blame him.

The drive down to Southampton went passing well. It was when it came to boarding that things started to go slightly awry. What neither of us realized was that we, or rather Bobby, would actually have to drive the car into the bowels of the boat. The last time we did this sort of thing was crossing to the Outer Hebrides for the salmon fishing. Then they simply put the thing in a large net and lifted the car on while Bobby was having an eye-opener in the bar.

There was a great deal of sign language from the sailor who was doing the loading and a great deal of bad language from Bobby. Fortunately there was no reversing so the thing was eventually done. Having held a licence from the days before you had to take a driving test Bobby is very good on a forward tack but quite hopeless when it comes to reversing.

After that we had to carry our hand luggage to our cabin ourselves. When we eventually found what turned out to be little more than a tiny cell, after what seemed like miles of tramping around in circles, it caused a new explosion. I really think that the old boy would have deserted the ship were it not that the car was now inextricably wedged bumper to bumper somewhere in the bilges.

The final shock came when we went in search of the bar and, hopefully, an invitation to dine later at the Captain's table. My Dear! Any notion of that sort was quickly dispelled. I know now that we were both expecting too much, remembering the old days on the dear old Star of India. After all, this is what is known as a one-class boat but to be faced with row upon row of gambling machines — those 'one-armed bandits' as Bertie calls that thing you put tenpenny pieces into at the Golf Club — but *hundreds* of them with *queues* of people waiting their turn! Those who were not at the machines were crowded three deep at the bar which by the time we found it was already *awash*.

No joy there so we set off without a great deal of pleasurable anticipation in search of the dining saloon. I will say this for it: it was clean, the hordes

"You can have his trousers
but not his Hawes and Curtis shirt!"

HAWES & CURTIS
2 Burlington Gardens
London W1
01-493 3803

having not yet descended. Nor, in fact, did it appear that the waiters had come on duty. We sat for quite a long time at a nice table by a porthole before it was borne in on me that it was 'self service'. You know, like they have in the basement at Harrod's. Bobby, surprisingly, was quite philosophical about this, saying that for some time now chaps were expected to help themselves to pudding at the Club.

In fact I managed to get not at all a bad bottle of wine to go with the bangers and mash (Bobby's favourite) and he showed distinct signs of rallying.

It was only when some of our fellow travellers started to straggle through from the bar that the clouds started to blow up again. Some of them were decidedly weaving on their feet, which I charitably put down to a very slight roll, but when a whole plate of fish and chips almost landed on Bobby's lap, I decided it was time to beat a dignified retreat.

The sun came out briefly as we passed through a sort of gaming saloon on the way to our quarters and one of the players literally *threw up* all over the green baize!

"That ought to shut the buggers up for the night!" said Bobby in a loud voice, grinning all over his face.

He is now lying flat on his back, mercifully sound asleep, whistling away through his nose like a widgeon, but I cannot disguise from you that I look forward to tomorrow morning when we are due to land on the Peninsula with some trepidation.

I hope that my next dispatch will reach you from Madrid where we are due to book in tomorrow night with the dear Potters. (He is now first secretary at the Embassy.)

Fond love,
Alice.

*   *   *

c/o The British Embassy,
Madrid.

Dear Mary,

Here we are again and this time very comfortable too, thank you. Not at all like that night we spent afloat, about which I hope you will have had my letter by now. Communications are not at all easy from here, but then are they from anywhere nowadays? I do think dear Mrs Thatcher made a mistake stopping us sending telegrams.

Well, the landing was comparatively uneventful. We went on deck after quite a decent breakfast. The boat was already in dock but our first view of Spain was unexciting — but then few sea ports are up to much, if you except Sydney.

Bobby was quite enchanted by the seabirds wheeling over the boat — particularly the kittiwakes whose wings seem almost translucent against the blue sky. Yes, the sky is really very blue and the weather more than clement.

While Bobby was gazing at the kittiwakes I looked down into the water and saw some most disgusting objects which were definitely *not* jelly fish — of which there were also plenty. Nobody could say that Bobby is a prude but visible evidence of this particular form of contraception is one of his aversions most likely to occasion an outburst — ever since he found one floating in the water butt outside the entrance to the greenhouses. (It was later traced to the gardener's boy and that was the end of *him*.)

Anyway, I didn't want him rushing round complaining to the Captain, the Bishop of Santander, Uncle Tom Cobbleigh and all, so I hurried him below on the pretext that we were about to disembark and we spent the next couple of hours (at least it seemed like a couple of hours) sitting in the ship's lounge, surrounded by hordes of trippers, most of whom, it

The English Gentleman has been informed — he cannot remember by whom — that smoking reduces the weight by as much as a third.

MOSTLY SMOKED

47 Elizabeth Street
London SW1 W9PP
Telephone 01-730 8367

appeared, were on some form of excursion and were only going ashore for a few hours before sampling the unalloyed joys of the return trip. Some of the wives looked quite exhausted already, poor dears, with their 'holiday break' not even half over.

When the time came we unloaded surprisingly rapidly and found ourselves in the port part of Santander desperately looking for the road signs to Madrid. I fear tempers got a bit short, particularly as Bobby insisted on driving on the 'wrong' side of the road.

When I pointed out that it is the accepted practice on the Continent to drive on the right of the road he replied that it was also generally accepted that all foreigners drive on the wrong side of the road and in his book two wrongs make a right.

Thus we continued through the centre of Santander to the accompaniment of much shouted abuse, whistles and waving of arms, so I was quite unable to concentrate on any of the city's architectural charms. So no reports about that.

It was a relief when we managed to get out of the city and came to a dual carriageway, when normal communications were restored between us.

So through the Cantabrian Mountains (most impressive) to a running commentary from Bobby on how the Iron Duke drove Napoleon out of the Peninsula. As always, I'm surprised how much Bobby knows about military matters and even as long ago as the Peninsular War, whenever that was. I got it mixed up with the Spanish Civil War and, trying to show intelligence, asked whose side General Franco had been on and got my head snapped off for my pains.

What with one thing and another (one of the 'anothers' was a rather protracted pit stop at a 'posada' where Bobby did some fairly thorough research into the merits of Spanish brandy) we arrived at the outskirts of Madrid in a high good humour.

English Gentlemen Abroad are advised not to omit
Twinings Teas from their inventory.

TWININGS
Teamen to Connoisseurs since 1706

.R. TWINING & CO LTD., SOUTHWAY, ANDOVER, HAMPSHIRE

Unfortunately, having once got onto the motorway we now found it almost impossible to get off it. We got onto what was evidently the equivalent of the Ring Road round Birmingham and everybody knows there is no way off *that*, even with the road signs in English.

On about the third time round Providence came to our rescue when I spotted a GB-plate motor-car drawn up in the forecourt of a garage and on enquiry we found that the driver was on his way not only to the centre of the city but to the very street in which the British Embassy was located. But for this stroke of luck we might still be circling the capital city of Spain like astronauts in a space shuttle which has lost its bleeps or whatever.

As it was we arrived exactly on time for the beginning of the post-siesta happy hour which is such a landmark in the day of our British expatriates.

Could you please ring Dobson and apologize for my omitting to give him the worm pills for Punch before I left. Tell him he will find them on the kitchen dresser in the jar marked 'ginger'.

In the meantime all our love to you and yours.

Alice

* * *

The Rock Hotel,
Gibraltar.

Dear Mary,

Forgive me for not having written before this. I am shocked to see that almost ten days have passed since I wrote from Madrid.

The truth is that I am having a most *difficult* time with Bobby. The thing is that he simply will *not* try to appreciate that he is in a foreign country with quite a different culture and sense of humour from our own. His 'Ho! Ho! Ho!' sort of jokes may be all very well in the smoking room at his beastly Blazers Club, but they are not appreciated by the highly sensitive and proud Spanish people and particularly when they are at their expense.

Of course I should have known when the dear Potters asked us to be their guests at a bull fight that trouble lay ahead and that I should have had one of my migranes but there: no point in crying over spilt milk and now we are safely back on British soil I suppose there were bits which were quite funny but most certainly not all!

Anyway, there we were seated in the very best seats right at the ringside below the Royal Box or whatever they call it and with only the narrowest of catwalks between us and the barricades. This was where all the matadors and people in their gorgeous costumes were collected when they were waiting for the first bull to appear. My dear! All those simply stunning young men in the tightest of tight trousers absolutely within touching distance! There I was positively droooling when one of them turned round and gave me the eye! I swear it! So handsome and with a costume which left absolutely *nothing* to the imagination.

In my excitement I must have accidentally nudged Bobby or something. Anyway he got out his monocle and gave the chap the once over. Then he brushed away at his moustache the way he has and went "harrumph". Wasn't it sweet?! I really think he was jealous!

Then this magnificent bull came charging into the ring. The matador or whatever was standing right in front of us and when the bull caught sight of him he came at him like an express train. He just gave a swirl of his cloak and stepped aside, whereupon the bull ran smack into the woodwork not three feet away from where we were sitting.

I am afraid I let out a rather girlish shriek and I was

"I just can't help wishing we were back in the Sloane Club!"

52 Lower Sloane Street
London SW1
Telephone 01-730 9131

not the only one. Bobby looked interested for the first time and inspected the animal which was pawing the ground in a fury of frustration, before leaning over me to ask Gervase Potter, "What d'ye think meat like that would fetch a pound in Smithfield Market?"

To give Bobby his due I think he really wanted to know, but I don't think Gerry took it too well.

Things thereafter did not get all that better. When the picadors came on, mounted on what was admittedly some not very high-class horse flesh it was hardly necessary for Bobby to remark that anyone turning up for a day's hunting with the Quorn mounted on bags of bone like that deserved to be reported to the Royal Society for the Prevention of Cruelty to Animals. It simply did not seem altogether appropriate in the circumstances. Still less when a really wicked-looking monster of a bull had knocked down my handsome admirer and Bobby got quite excited and forgot himself to the extreme of shouting, "Watch it or you'll get a horn up your Khyber Pass." He can be dreadfully vulgar at times. I only hope that Rosie Potter, who has never been married to an army man, did not understand the anatomical reference.

Really, all things considered, we did not leave Madrid under too much of a cloud, although when Gerry offered to lend Bobby a road map I did have just the teeniest suspicion that perhaps we might be in danger of outstaying our welcome. Bobby, however, was in the highest of spirits and at once started to make plans to re-route ourselves through Portugal — not as everyone at first suspected so that he could call in at Oporto which is, as you know, the H.Q. of the Port trade and only English is spoken, but to visit the old battlefield called Torres Vedras where he claims that his great-great-great-Uncle Willie captured that vulgar French sword he insists on hanging above the loo in the gun-room.

Fortunately a note from his old friend 'Pongo' Forsyth caught up with us via the diplomatic bag, inviting us to stay with he and dear Betty and promising a 'decent drop of the old Stuff', so we set off hot foot.

What a delight to be among English-speaking natives again and to be saluted by British-uniformed police (even if their skins are a bit olive-coloured).

My dearest love to you all. Please tell Benson to rush six boxes of *thin* extra strong loo paper by airmail but to be sure to take it out of the boxes first to save unnecessary expense.

We shall hope to start on the homeward leg early next week. Bobby refuses to go on that steamer again so there is talk of driving all the way back via Biarritz where our address will be c/o The English Club, 69 Rue Edouard Sept, Biarritz, Pays Basque, France.

Devotedly,
Alice

*   *   *

The Hotel Reine Victoria
Rue Edouard Sept,
Biarritz, France. P.B.

Dear Mary,

Gibraltar was the greatest success. Quite splendidly British in the best traditions of the Empire. Bobby was, of course, absolutely in his element, snapping to attention every time a bugle sounded, or the Governor drove past or he spotted a Union Jack, which, you can imagine, was pretty well all the time.

In fact Bobby got so carried away that he swore he would never sleep in a foreign bed again. He and Pongo Forsyth sat round the dinner table into the small hours with the port decanter rocketing back and forward between them like a ping-pong ball whilst they marked out in red all the places in Europe where

a chap could stay in civilized surroundings and marking them with a red dot.

It would appear that going back up the East coast of Spain (Bobby has refused to get on that boat again) the nearest 'safe house' is the English Club at Biarritz just over the French frontier. Too far for a one-day drive and Bobby has absolutely refused to stay in one of those Spanish Hostels which everyone who has tried them say are absolutely marvellous and inexpensive.

For a time it looked as if the only way out was by a Hercules aircraft or perhaps a gun-boat. Then luckily Pongo remembered an old friend who had been in the Regiment who had quite a nice little place near Valencia and he fixed us up there. It meant driving like billy-oh the next day to make Biarritz by dinner time.

Biarritz is really rather sweet with lots of splendid Victorian-mansion-type villas, like Bognor Regis on a sunny day. All the streets are named after our royal family except those called after the Princess Eugenie who had Napoleon III build a monstrously ornate summer palace for her — later the Hotel du Palais where Edward VII was wont to romp with his assorted ladies of the bedchamber.

They are all immensely pro-British, although none of them seem to speak a word of English. This does not worry Bobby because he likes to show off his French when ever possible. As the number of phrases at his command is severely limited this calls for considerable ingenuity on my part on creating situations where he can order someone to bring him the pen of his aunt and so on.

Unfortunately my efforts to give him an opportunity to display his fluent command of the language tend to backfire, like yesterday morning when he took me for a stroll along the front and stopped off at a cafe before he made a bolt for the English Club.

Putting on my helpless-little-me act I asked him how I should order a strawberry ice. This got him a little bit out of his depth so, to gain time, he patted my hand and said, "Look it up in your phrase book". By the sheerest bad luck, he suddenly remembered that the French for strawberry was 'fraise' and that he had unwittingly made a quite appalling pun. Naturally he does not see it that way and he has already retailed this evidence of his bilingual wit four times with appropriate explanation — 'phrase', 'fraise' get it? — while beating the air and rolling about helpless with laughter.

I fear that the life expectancy of this joke may be regarded as almost indefinite, so be prepared against the hour of our return.

With regard to the English Club it appeared, rather unfortunately in my view, that the wind of change had been blowing and ladies are now admitted to partake of tea and muffins on Saturday afternoons. Well, I suppose it makes a change from reading year-old copies of the Tatler and Field in the Golf clubhouse, so I went along.

Talk about some corner of a foreign field being forever England! It could be Blazers to a T, right down to the smell of damp cabbage and the moth holes in the green baize of the bridge tables.

I ran into Molly Pargetter who was in the same form as me at Cheltenham. She spotted me first and let out the sort of whoop with which the survivors must have greeted their rescuers at the relief of Mafeking. Not that old Molly looked all that starved or down-in-the-mouth. Quite the contrary, she looked the picture of health and still gave the impression that she was about to bully-off in a hockey match, which I remember so well. It was just a natural reaction to seeing a new face and, looking round at some of the old fogies dozing off in the leather armchairs dotted around in the smoking-room I could guess how she felt.

She told me that things had quietened down a lot since the local hunt had packed up and everyone had had to put their pink coats into store. She also told me that she and her husband never come back to England now that his old nanny is dead and that the only trip they make is once a year to Paris for the Arc de Triomphe at Longchamps, and a bit of a knees up afterwards at the Jockey Club.

The Jockey have reciprocal arrangements with Bobby's Blazer's so that is to be the next safe house. We seem to be using up those red spots quite fast.

Anyway it looks like home for us by the end of the week. Would you give Dobson a warning order of our return. I do hope he has not found the key of the wine cellar.

I will telegraph you of our E.T.A. and do come round *immediately* so that Bobby can get his 'fraise' story off his chest.

Fond love
Alice.

Islands in the Sun

Of all places abroad which changing fashions may recommend, by far the most constant in the affections of gentleman are islands.

Why this should be so is not entirely clear. It could be something to do with our own island heritage but it is certainly deep-seated. Gentleman regard islands not only as places to visit on holiday but as places where a fellow can decently retire to when the blood starts to run too thin in the veins to contemplate another winter in a freezing cold mansion.

Ever since Drake and Raleigh set forth on their voyages of discovery the British have developed a passion for collecting islands with a dedication unmatched in the history of the civilized world.

It only required a wandering mariner to sight a coral-girt atoll thousands of miles from anywhere and inhabited only by goats and sea turtles for him to stick a Union Jack on it and claim it in the name of the Monarch. This typically British idiosyncrasy has caused great embarrassment to successive British Governments and, not least, to Mrs Thatcher's.

It might not come amiss here to look at one or two of the most favoured islands to try and detect some common standard by which this extraordinary island-fixation can be explained.

*A visit to a reputable London cigar merchant might
be considered prudent before setting out overseas –*

even in contemplation of a day trip to Boulogne.

Madeira

Certainly part of the fascination which the island of Madeira has always held for the British springs from the frustration of knowing that it should have been British by right.

When Catherine of Braganza became affianced to our own Charles II, the Portuguese tried to swing Madeira on him as part of her dowry. As at the time the island consisted of little of anything, the offer was refused and Charles settled for more cash in lieu.

Just the same some very long-headed Scottish gentlemen went to have a look and before you could say Auchtermuchty they had set the islanders to work to produce the splendid Madeira wine so beloved by the Victorians, exquisite lacework and much else besides.

They also made it one of the most fashionable of winter resorts, built that splendid pile Reid's Hotel in their own image, and founded the English Club with muffins for afternoon tea and anyone for tennis. Not to belong to the English Club was to be nobody.

The resolute determination of Reid's Hotel, a sister hotel to Shepheard's in Cairo, to produce traditional English fare with turkey on Christmas day, to be followed by plum pudding with the crackers made a nice change for the regulars who were apt to get bored with roast beef and two veg. on all the other days of the year. The difficulty of serving decent fish was overcome by introducing the *espada*, deemed a great local delicacy, which, in the opinion of most, tastes like rather poor quality newsprint, was always regarded with tolerance as evidence of a rather charming eccentricity.

Today the English grip is not so much relaxing as becoming threatened by the package-tour brigade and a resulting plethora of resort-type hotels which tends to weaken the stiff-upper-lip image.

In the high season there are a few nervous glances towards the door of the English Club for fear some damned fellow in an open-necked shirt should show up demanding admittance and complaints that the narrow streets of Funchal proliferate petrol fumes where in a more spacious time progress was by peasant-pulled sledges.

On the whole, however, there is a quiet confidence that the status quo is in no real danger.

Corfu

Corfu has the same place in the affections of the English Gentleman as Madeira and perhaps with better reason as we really did once own it. We took it away from Napoleon, whom we sent off to Elba, and ran it for quite a while before giving it back to the Greeks who had owned it since Shakespeare's Prospero had his cave there and Homer visited it for weekends.

Naturally we did not hand it back in the condition in which we had found it. We left behind one of the finest British cemeteries to join the tradition of fine British cemeteries all over the world, a cricket pitch in the centre of Corfu town which remains a Mecca for islanders and visitors alike and an abiding love amongst the Corfiots for ginger beer.

More recently, like so many other places where a chap could find a bit of peace and quiet, Corfu has become invaded by hordes of package tourists and the coastline dotted with holiday complexes of various degrees of luxury. Worse, in the eyes of the many inclined-to-be elderly English residents there has been an alarming outbreak of nudity on the beaches with topless typists competing with each other in displaying the amplitude of the charms which they keep so assiduously concealed for the other fifty weeks of the year in our more temperate clime.

[78]

The attitude of the true-blue Brits has been to
retreat further and further into the hinterland so that
some of the more remote villages in the hills have become literally a-crackle with whalebone corsets and
snapping lorgnettes. The natives knuckle their
foreheads as they sweep by as regular as minute guns
to take tiffin with one another and not a few make the
sign of the Holy Cross but by and large the English
community is still regarded with the same affection as
in the days of yore.

Sri Lanka

It is really a question of whether Sri Lanka, by the
simple expedient of changing its name from Ceylon,
did enough to be considered as Abroad by the British.

There has always been, of course, a firm line drawn
in the minds of most people between our erstwhile
Colonies and Abroad. Abroad is inhabited by foreigners but places like India, large parts of Africa and
other red spots around the world have always been
considered part of one happy family, with the servants, naturally kept affectionately but firmly in their
place.

It is probably true to say that, certainly in the eyes of
the British, little has changed with the lowering of the
Union Jack over the Hill Club at Nuwara Eliya,
despite some insensitive jokes about it being referred
to as the over-the-hill Club.

Indeed it would be true to say that, with the with-
drawal of our administrators, the hard core of true
Brit residents has increased and the traditional eccen-
tricities expected of the British gentleman resident
abroad conscientiously (perhaps even a trifle self-
consciously) upheld.

Somebody once remarked that in the days of the
Raj, English society in Ceylon refused to recognise
that it was an island off the southern tip of India but

"*Of course we're not on a package tour –*
we may be broke but we still have the two Pegasus!"

PEGASUS TRANSPORT SYSTEMS LTD
Hatfield, Hertfordshire

regarded it rather as being somewhere a few miles from Godalming. Perhaps today it has even gone a little up-market in social acceptance, just down the road from Belgravia perhaps.

It all has something to do with those airplanes...

That last line about airplanes suddenly reared up and kicked me.

Great Heavens! Could it be that improved communications and a lessening of the traditional tensions between ourselves and our late Colonies on the other side of the Atlantic Ocean could have become so settled after two major conflicts as Allies-in-arms as to rate alongside some of the other destinations mentioned in this book as 'good places to go'? After all, the blood ties are strong, the historical association unquestionable and we have had a lot of them over here either to have a shot at our enemies in stern times of war or at our grouse and pheasants in the sometimes sterner times of peace.

Could there now be a time when a reverse traffic might be established? And established to such an extent as to deserve a place in this book?

Now it will be noted that this work is published by the ancient and much revered publishing house of Burke's Peerage and, by one of those very English contradictions in terms, its editorial destiny is controlled by a thinly-disguised American, a Mr Harold Brooks-Baker.

By this time the depth of my own researches had resulted in my being considerably bogged down in a prolonged *séjour* at the Negresco Hotel in Nice. The work had been onerous. By night I was observing the geographical distribution of the English Gentleman in his former well-established nesting sites along that particular part of the Mediterranean Coast, while by day my studies were of an even more ornithological nature — spotting the increasingly prevalent Greater

German Brown Tit basking on the beaches and the elusive Smaller English White Tit flitting shyly on the less populated stretches.

Understandably exhausted and emotional, I wrote to H.B.B. saying I could go no further and handing on to him the sacred flame of the search-after-truth.

Could it be? I asked... and who? and where? Does he? Can we? Should we?

Swiftly the answer came.

* * *

Dear Douglas,

You do ask the strangest questions in your letter. As you should well know Gentlemen never go abroad except possibly to visit their mistresses or attend funerals. Abroad is anywhere East of Dover or North of Maryland. Your own dear late friend, Nancy Mitford, made this very clear: "I loathe Abroad, nothing would induce me to live there... as for foreigners they make me sick." (Uncle Matthew in *The Pursuit of Love*). However, the American South is perfectly safe for you because it is merely an extension of the British Isles.

But, my dear Douglas, when you come, by steamer or airplane, be very careful not to land North of Maryland. Those Northern Lands are peopled by descendants of the so-called Pilgrims — who live like oysters, surrounded by icebergs. They are all second-rate industrialists, or long to be so, constantly changing houses and Presidents.

Our ancestors, who came to this continent after the Settlement of Jamestown Colony, were Gentlemen, the sons of The Landed Gentry or Aristocrats. We always live in the same Antebellum mansion and are delighted that our only President, Jefferson Davis, cannot be improved upon.

[82]

However, even safe in the S.S.A. (Southern States of America) you must continue to be wary. Be careful not to accept invitations from people who pretend they are Southern Gentlemen. These people are generally Yankees or foreigners. You can always recognize these rascals by their smart, off-the-peg clothes and their sparkling shining houses. New clothes on a man and fresh paint on a house are always danger signals. There are also Europeans and Englishmen (who are often not Gentlemen) busy looking for plantations to use as second homes. These are easily spotted by the Initials or Coats of Arms on the mailboxes.

A film crew was here recently making a series on Lady Astor who was born in Virginia. The Director observed that the people and countryside reminded him of England. "Isn't that what you expect of a Colony?" replied their host, Colonel Randolph Randolph.

In Britain you have the system of U & Non-U to protect you from Untouchables. Here we have another code, F.F.V. However, in the fear that a latter-day Nancy Mitford might reveal all to the masses, only We know the meaning of those letters.

So Douglas, do come soon. Avoid the pitfalls and the icebergs of the North, and I promise you that here in the S.S.A. you won't even realize that you are away from Home.

Love,
Brookie

H.B. Brooks-Baker, Publishing Director, Burke's Peerage, Charlottesville, Va.

Moving with the Times

Were the English Gentleman the reactionary fuddy-duddy he is often made out to be there is no doubt that as a species he would have long ago ceased to exist. The brontosaurus and the pterodactyl failed to adapt and have long perished from the earth. Nothing like that is going to happen to the English Gentleman if he can help it. It is something he has been working on for many years now and there are few more apposite examples of this ability to adapt to changing conditions than in the field of foreign travel in general and foreigners in particular.

Foreign Relations

The growing touchiness in the world over ethnic distinctions has not escaped the English Gentleman. He has never referred to coloured folk, for example, as 'Niggers' or 'Nig-Nogs', such terms being the prerogative of the socially insecure, and he will readily desist from using such names as 'Sambo' or 'Golly' when it has been pointed out to him that such affectionate endearments from his nursery days have come to be considered as racially offensive.

It should be remarked here that the English Gentleman has always been neutral in the Black versus White controversy which seems to have become so

*The English Gentleman and Pol Roger champagne –
the peak of achievement.*

much more heated since the 'do-gooders' have taken a hand.

In fact there has never been a time when a gentleman would have refused to ask a fellow to his club purely on account of his colour. That so few did can be fairly put down to lack of opportunity. That one who did so recently at my own club should have seen fit to apologise in a loud voice for there being no missionary soup on the menu should simply be put down to his sense of fun.

Frogs and Krauts

This sensitivity regarding the familiar nomenclature of the coloured races does not apply when we get nearer home. It should be remembered that a habit all gentlemen have is to give everyone for whom they have the slightest affection some sort of nickname and generally the ruder and the more appropriate the more affectionate. "Tubby", "Stinker" and "Bugger Lugs" are examples of the sort of fond sobriquets, often bestowed in early school days, which last on into later life.

Within the compass of this sceptered isle the racial distinctions are usually grouped together under such generic descriptions as "Micks", "Jocks" or "Taffys" — and particularly if they should enjoy the social distinction of belonging to the Brigade of Guards — so the average English Gentleman finds it hard to understand why, for example, Germans in the mass should object to being described as "Krauts" or the French as "Frogs".

It is perhaps worth observing that there is no similarly affectionate nickname for the purely English and one can only hazard a guess why this should be so.

The Wardrobe

Further evidence of the English Gentleman's willingness to adapt is seen in his dress.

It is perhaps worth observing that there is no similarly affectionate nickname for the purely English and one can only hazard a guess why this should be so.

The Wardrobe

Further evidence of the English Gentleman's willingness to adapt is in the matter of dress.

It is no longer considered obligatory when travelling abroad to carry a rolled umbrella or wear a bowler hat, except of course when attending a race meeting or calling upon the Ambassador.

Similarly it is quite normal for gentlemen nowadays when dining out not to change into a dinner jacket. A dark suit is considered perfectly appropriate. The fact that even this concession to informality still renders him distinctive in an increasingly cosmopolitan society does not concern him. It is not his ambition to be cosmopolitan.

An even more marked revolution in the matter of dress has taken place among the younger English ladies. The days when it was unthinkable to travel as far as Frinton-on-Sea without adequate protection against the rays of the sun are now long since past. It is no longer *de rigueur* to shade the delicate English complexion under parasols and enormous flowered hats. This bronze-is-beautiful revolution means that ladies can now go on their foreign travels without a hat box in sight and most of their other needs for a holiday in the sun can be carried in a beauty case of the most modest proportions. Truly a revolution from the not-so-far-distant days of the English Memsahib.

In and Out

Nothing demonstrates the flexibility of the modern English Gentleman's attitude to abroad more than his willingness to desert the haunts of his father and his father's father and discover pastures new.

"You never said you'd asked Fortnums to lay on a hamper!"

Fortnum & Mason
Piccadilly London W1A 1ER. Telephone 01-734 8040

This capriciousness is made all the more remarkable by the unanimity with which new places are declared as being 'In' or 'Out'. In this they resemble nothing more than a flock of starlings which, if one takes a new direction, all the rest of the flock make exactly the same turn, actuated by heaven knows what instinct. It is in sharp contrast to the habits of their forebears who plodded stolidly round the never-varying circuit.

Today the Channel resorts are decidedly out. Le Touquet has never recovered from such well-loved watering holes as the Picardy and the Golf being reduced to rubble in 1944 or Deauville, which remained intact, from remaining so stubbornly Victorian.

Indeed the devotion of the French to the shades of the peripatetic Victorians has dealt many a French resort a body-blow from which they look unlikely to recover — the aforementioned Biarritz, for example, and its neighbour Saint Jean de Luz.

For that matter the English milords are nowadays pretty thin on the ground in their once prime stamping grounds like Monte Carlo and Cannes, driven out for the most part by the influx of rich Greeks on their yachts and film starlets on their backs, not to mention the Arabs, the Germans and all the rest of the international kittle-kattle.

Places like Marbella in the South of Spain, of course, never got off the ground, the fleeing financiers and playboys of the Western World having got there first.

Switzerland is, of all places in Europe, the place where the English Gentleman is at his most chameleon. St Moritz, where the English Gentleman used to go in considerable numbers for the sledging and curling, has long suffered the same fate as large parts of the South of France at the hands of the dreaded inter-

national set, but the smaller ski-resorts higher up the
mountains enjoy sudden periods of popularity. It is,
however, the comparatively newly developed resorts
in the French Alps, like Meribel-les-Allues, where the
most aristocratic go to frolic in the snow. The Italian
Alps, too, are 'in', particularly with the younger set,
and attract planes full of Etonian schoolboys. A good
word should also be said for Austria with places like
Innsbruck currently in high favour with the energetic
and Oberammergau for the less eccentric. A bad word
for Germany where most of the once fashionable
Bads like Bad Homburg and Bad Martzberg do not
seem to have staged much of a recovery and Stras-
bourg is of course stuck with all those European
Parliamentarians. Only Baden Baden retains some of
the trails of glory from its past.

* * *

And so. Soyer le beinconnu. Whol kommen. Arrive-
derchi or see you again...
    I'll see you again
    Somewhere
    I don't know when
    But I'll see you again
    Some sunny day....
Oh, Golly Gosh! I do hope so!
....but I sometimes wonder do the French, the
Germans, the Spanish, the Dutch, the Italians and all
the rest?

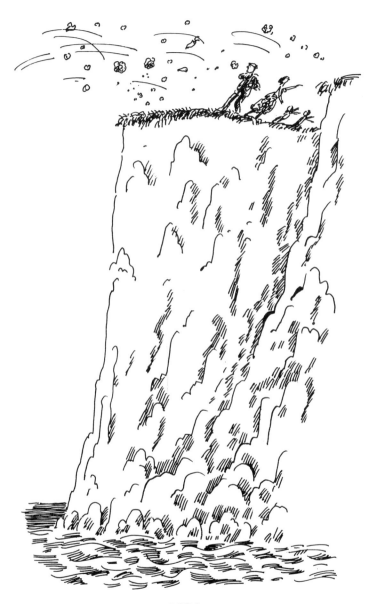